Showdown

Olympic Spirit

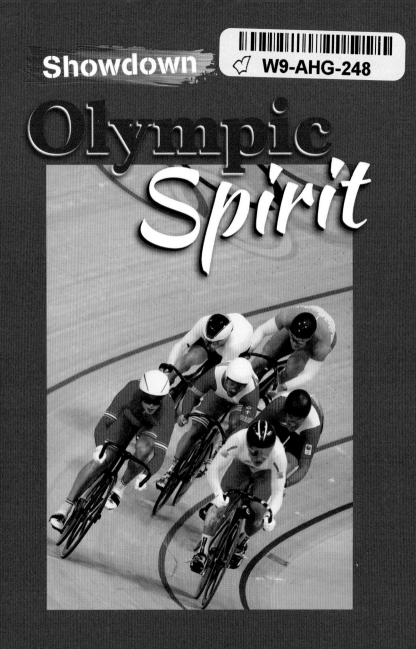

Ben Nussbaum

Publishing Credits

Rachelle Cracchiolo, *M.S.Ed., Publisher*
Conni Medina, M.A.Ed., *Managing Editor*
Nika Fabienke, Ed.D., *Series Developer*
June Kikuchi, *Content Director*
Susan Daddis, M.A.Ed., *Editor*
Kevin Pham, *Graphic Designer*

The TIME logo is a registered trademark of TIME Inc. Used under license.

Image Credits: Front cover, p.1 Petr Toman/Shutterstock; p.1
(background) BBA Photography/Shutterstock; pp.8–9 Aflo Co., Ltd./
Alamy; pp.10–11 Action Plus Sports/Alamy; p.15 (bottom right) Xinhua/
Alamy; pp.16–17 Tim Clayton/Corbis via Getty Images; pp.18–19 James
Whitmore/The LIFE Picture Collection/Getty Images; p.20 Mark Kauffman/
The LIFE Picture Collection/Getty Images; p.22 (middle) Popperfoto/
Getty Images; p.24 (top) Li Ming/Xinhua/Alamy; pp.24–25 Mario Tama/
Getty Images; pp.26–27 Yasuyoshi Chiba/AFP/Getty Images; p.28 (bottom)
Urbanbuzz/Shutterstock; pp.30–31 Mike Powell /Allsport/Getty Images;
p.34 (bottom) James Davie/Alamy; pp.34–35 George S. de Blonsky/Alamy;
p.36 Scott Barbour/Allsport/Getty Images; pp.36–37 Bob Daemmrich/
Alamy; pp.38–39 Santiago Vidal Vallejo/Alamy; pp.40–41 Odd Andersen/
AFP/Getty Images; all other images from iStsock and or Shutterstock.

Library of Congress Cataloging-in-Publication Data

Names: Nussbaum, Ben, 1975- author.
Title: Showdown : Olympics / Ben Nussbaum.
Description: Huntington Beach, CA : Teacher Created Materials, 2019. |
  Includes index. | Audience: Grade 4 to 6.
Identifiers: LCCN 2017056312 (print) | LCCN 2018010926 (ebook) | ISBN
  9781425849993 (e-book) | ISBN 9781425849993 (pbk.)
Subjects: LCSH: Olympics–Juvenile literature. | Sportsmanship–Juvenile
  literature.
Classification: LCC GV721.53 (ebook) | LCC GV721.53 .N87 2019 (print) | DDC
  796.48–dc23
LC record available at https://lccn.loc.gov/2017056312

Teacher Created Materials
5301 Oceanus Drive
Huntington Beach, CA 92649-1030
www.tcmpub.com
ISBN 978-1-4258-4999-3
© 2019 Teacher Created Materials, Inc.
Printed in Malaysia
Thumbprints.22064

Table of Contents

Olympic Ideals

Can sports make the world a better place? Pierre de Coubertin (duh koo-behr-TEHN) thought so. The French educator had big dreams—and a very specific plan. Inspired by ancient Greek sporting events that brought together rival cities, he wanted to create an athletic festival that would bring together the whole world.

In 1896, his vision gave birth to the first modern Olympics. They were held in Athens, Greece.

De Coubertin did not organize the Olympics just to find out who could run the fastest or who could jump the farthest. In a poem, de Coubertin captured the spirit he wanted for the Olympics. "O sport, you are peace! You **forge** happy bonds between people," he wrote.

For over one hundred years, the Olympics have brought people together, proving that competition can create community.

Olympic Art?

From 1912 to 1948, the Olympics included an art competition. Mixing art and sports was part of de Coubertin's unique vision. De Coubertin even won a gold medal for his poem "Ode to Sport."

Pierre de Coubertin

All-Around Sportsman

De Coubertin was passionate about rugby. He was inducted into the World Rugby Hall of Fame for his work promoting the sport.

A Global Gathering

Athletes from 14 nations entered the first Games. The Olympics have grown in size ever since. The 2016 Summer Olympics in Rio de Janeiro played host to athletes from more than 200 nations. Almost every country in the world sent at least one athlete to Rio.

Spectators travel from around the world come to cheer at the Games, too. Half a million foreigners went to Rio to watch the Games. The city was happy to welcome such **diversity.**

About 3.5 billion people watched the Rio Games on television. That's half the people in the world! For comparison, about 100 million people watch the Super Bowl each year. More than any other event, the Olympics truly unite the planet.

Bringing Home the Cup

Soccer's World Cup is the only event that rivals the Olympics in terms of worldwide excitement. There's one big difference, though. Only 32 countries qualify for the World Cup.

One highlight of the Olympics is the opening ceremony. It gives the host nation a chance to welcome the world.

The 2008 Summer Olympics in Beijing kicked off in style. A huge cast put on an incredible show. The ceremony celebrated China's past and present. It showed off China's invention of **gunpowder**, paper, and the **compass**. It highlighted China's **philosophers** and traditional music. It also showed China's ethnic diversity.

An announcer captured the spirit of the event: "The world has given its love and trust to China, and today China will give the world a big, warm hug."

The Olympic Games are a break from conflict. They are a chance for the world to feel united.

Spectacular Spectacle

Beijing's opening ceremony cost about $100 million. That is more than twice the amount spent four years earlier in Athens. Beijing's ceremony was four hours long and included about 15,000 performers. Drums that lit up as they were played dazzled viewers around the world!

2008 Opening Ceremony
in Beijing

9

The Olympics can even help divided countries heal. In 1992, Germany sent one team to the Games for the first time in decades. West Germany and East Germany had been separate countries. They were in the midst of coming together. It was not an easy process.

The Olympics gave the nation a chance to celebrate unity. "It is the place for sports to lead in this direction. It is a great step towards peace," explained Joachim Weiskopf, the head of the East German Olympic Committee.

Boycott Blues

In 1980, the United States did not take part in the Moscow Olympics. President Jimmy Carter made the decision. The former Soviet Union had invaded Afghanistan and would not withdraw its troops. Four years later, the Soviet Union hit back. It **boycotted** the Olympics in Los Angeles.

At some recent Olympics, North Korea and South Korea have marched together in the opening ceremony. The athletes have waved the flag of a **unified** Korea. This gesture is symbolic, but it is still important. It gives Koreans a glimpse of what their two countries can hope for someday.

2014 Closing Ceremony of the Winter Games in Sochi, Russia

Welcome Back

South Africa was banned from the Olympics for many years. Its **apartheid** system was built on racism. In 1992, after South Africa reformed, it came back to the Olympics. This was a huge victory for South African athletes!

The Olympics: A Big Deal

The Summer and Winter Olympics have both grown dramatically. At almost every Olympic Games, there are more athletes from more countries taking part in more events.

Summer Olympics

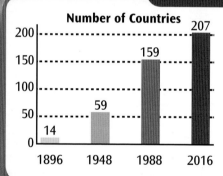

Number of Countries

- 1896: 14
- 1948: 59
- 1988: 159
- 2016: 207

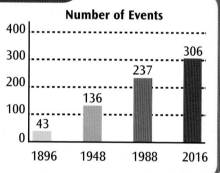

Number of Events

- 1896: 43
- 1948: 136
- 1988: 237
- 2016: 306

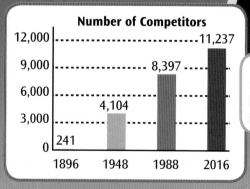

Number of Competitors

- 1896: 241
- 1948: 4,104
- 1988: 8,397
- 2016: 11,237

Athens, Greece, 1896
London, England, 1948
Seoul, South Korea, 1988
Rio de Janeiro, Brazil, 2016

Winter Olympics

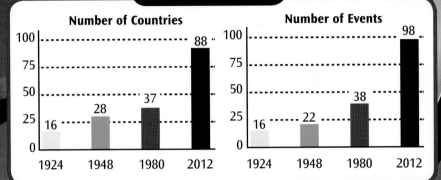

Number of Countries

Year	Value
1924	16
1948	28
1980	37
2012	88

Number of Events

Year	Value
1924	16
1948	22
1980	38
2012	98

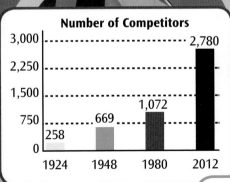

Number of Competitors

Year	Value
1924	258
1948	669
1980	1,072
2012	2,780

Chamonix, France, 1924
St. Moritz, Switzerland, 1948
Lake Placid, NY, USA, 1980
Sochi, Russia, 2012

All-Around Champs

At the Olympics, the spirit of community extends to the competitors. In many cases, athletes train for years to become Olympians. During this **grueling** process, they form close friendships. Sometimes, they end up competing against their friends.

Raisman performs on the beam in 2016.

Grandma Aly

Raisman's teammates kidded her by calling her "grandma." Even though she was only 22, she was the oldest member of the gymnastics team. She helped the other athletes stay calm and focused.

Golden Girls

In 2016, United States gymnasts gave the world a vivid example of the Olympic spirit. Only two gymnasts from each country are allowed to advance to the individual all-around competition. Simone Biles had already qualified. Gabby Douglas and Aly Raisman had to compete for the other American spot.

Douglas and Raisman had both been members of the 2012 Olympic team. They had spent years training together. They were friends. But now, they were rivals.

Douglas wrapped up her events first. Raisman had only one event left.

Sibling Rivalry

Competing against a friend can be hard. Imagine competing against your sisters! The Luik triplets from Estonia competed in the 2016 Rio women's marathon. In the same race, the Hahner twins, from Germany, crossed the finish line holding hands.

Douglas and Raisman hug after winning the gold medal as a team.

Serious Dedication

Olympic gymnasts train about 30 hours a week. Sometimes, they even move away from their families to be closer to their coaches.

If Raisman nailed her routine on the beam, she would take the second American spot in the all-around competition. Douglas would not be able to compete and defend her all-around gold medal from 2012.

As Raisman performed, Douglas watched **attentively**. If Raisman fell from the beam—or even if she bobbled and touched the beam with her hand—Douglas would advance.

But Douglas did not cheer for Raisman to make a mistake. Instead, she smiled as her teammate performed well. When Raisman nailed her landing, Douglas was the first person to give her a hug.

"They did an amazing job and they deserve it. ...I'm so happy for them," Douglas said about Biles and Raisman, who went on to win the gold and silver medals.

Love on Ice

Sometimes, romantic partners compete together at the Olympics. Chinese pair skaters Tong Jian and Pang Qing trained together for almost 20 years. They won the silver medal at the 2010 Olympics. The next year, they got engaged!

Dynamic Duo

At the 1960 Summer Olympics, **decathletes** Rafer Johnson and C.K. Yang inspired two nations. Johnson was American and Yang was from Taiwan, but they trained together in Los Angeles.

Johnson helped Yang get used to America. "From the very beginning, we hit it off," he explained. He took Yang to his own home on weekends, where Johnson's mom prepared healthy food for the young athletes. Yang even went to church with the Johnsons.

Johnson

World's Greatest Athlete

The 1912 Olympics were held in Sweden. Jim Thorpe was an American Indian competing for the United States. He was entered in the **pentathlon** and decathlon. He won gold medals in both, destroying his competition.

Soon, Johnson and Yang developed into two of the best decathletes in the entire world. When Johnson was severely hurt in a 1959 car crash, it could have helped Yang. It meant one less competitor for the gold medal. But Yang did everything he could to help his friend recover.

A Country's Hope

Yang had added pressure. Taiwan had never won a medal. He represented the hopes of the entire country.

Yang

At the Olympics in Rome, the two men had an amazing duel. The lead went back and forth during the grueling two-day, ten-event decathlon.

The final event was the 1,500-meter run, a test of endurance and **fortitude**. If Yang could beat Johnson by 10 seconds, he would win gold. Yang pulled ahead, but Johnson stayed close behind. Crossing the finish line, both men were utterly exhausted. On the verge of collapsing, the first thing they did was embrace each other. Johnson's performance in the race earned him gold, while Yang took home silver.

Their Olympic careers united Johnson and Yang instead of driving them apart. "Sports is about opening your heart to others," Yang explained.

Check out how Johnson and Yang did in each of the events at the 1960 Olympics. Bronze medalist Vasili Kuznetsov's results are also shown. There were 30 competitors in the decathlon. The table shows how the three medalists ranked in each event.

	Johnson	Yang	Kuznetsov
100-meter race	3	1	4
Long jump	2	1	6
Shot put	1	14	4
High jump	3	1	16
400-meter race	3	2	6
110-meter hurdles	5	1	4
Discus throw	3	11	1
Pole vault	3	1	5
Javelin throw	3	4	2
1,500-meter race	15	12	16

> Do you think it's fair that Yang won the silver medal even though he did better than Johnson in most of the events? Why or why not?

> How did Kuznetsov's performance compare?

The Olympic Rings

The Olympic logo is full of messages about unity and togetherness.
Designed by Pierre de Coubertin, it was first used in 1914 to celebrate
the 20th anniversary of the International Olympic Committee.

De Coubertin originally drew the logo with the five rings in a row. It quickly changed to the current version, with three rings on top and two on the bottom.

The five rings represent the five continents that send athletes to the Olympics. (De Coubertin counted North and South America as one continent.) They are linked together to show how the Olympics unite the world.

The five colors were chosen because they are commonly used in flags of the world. According to de Coubertin, every nation that had competed in the Olympics up to 1931 used only these colors (along with white) in their flag.

Each Olympic Games has its own logo that features the Olympic rings.

Silver and Copper?

Today, the Olympics give out gold, silver, and bronze medals to the top three athletes in each event. At the 1896 Olympics in Athens, first-place winners received a silver medal. People who came in second place received a copper medal.

Mardini trains hard before the 2016 Games.

Unlikely Winners

"The most important thing in the Olympic Games is not to win, but to take part. The essential thing in life is not conquering but fighting well," de Coubertin wrote.

At every Olympics, a few athletes are thrown into the spotlight. They remind the world that the Olympics are a celebration of community. They also teach that winning is about doing your best.

A True Champion

The 2016 Rio Olympics gave the world a new hero in swimmer Yusra Mardini. She swam for Syria before her family's home was destroyed in a civil war. She became part of the Refugee Olympic Team (ROT). The team was made up of athletes who were displaced from their home countries. They competed under the Olympic flag.

Medal Ceremonies

For many years, medals were handed out at the end of the Olympics. Many athletes had already gone home! A medal ceremony at the end of each event was added in 1932.

Mardini fled her home country in 2015. During her dangerous journey to safety, she was on a small boat crowded with other refugees when the motor stopped working. The **dinghy** threatened to **capsize**. Mardini jumped into the water and, swimming, pushed the boat to shore. "I thought it would be a real shame if I drowned in the sea, because I am a swimmer," she remembered thinking.

In Germany, she found a coach and resumed training. At the Olympics, she won an early **heat**, delighting the crowd in Rio.

"I want to make all the refugees proud of me. It would show that, even if we had a tough journey, we can achieve something," Mardini said.

Competing for the World

In 2016, the first team made up of refugees went to Rio to compete. Ten athletes were on the ROT. They all left their home countries because of war. They represented an estimated 65 million refugees around the world. That number is almost equal to the population of France.

The ROT takes a picture together in front of a landmark statue in Rio.

Fly Like an Eagle

Eddie "the Eagle" Edwards competed in the ski jump at the 1988 Winter Olympics in Calgary, Canada. Before Edwards, Great Britain did not have a ski-jumping team. In fact, Britain did not have any ski jumpers at all!

Edwards was not **sponsored**. The British Olympic Committee did not support him. He trained abroad and made do with secondhand equipment.

Edwards did not look like a ski jumper. He wore thick glasses that misted up on the jump hill, making it difficult for him to see as he landed.

Despite his nickname, Eddie the Eagle did not soar. He finished in last place at the Olympics. He still became a great Olympic hero. People around the world cheered for him because of his determination and can-do attitude.

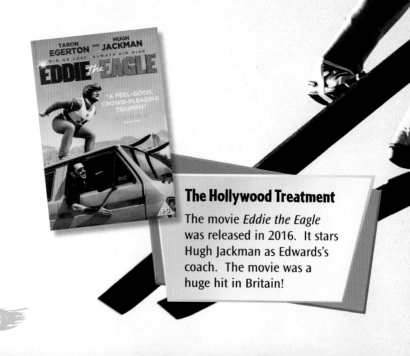

The Hollywood Treatment

The movie *Eddie the Eagle* was released in 2016. It stars Hugh Jackman as Edwards's coach. The movie was a huge hit in Britain!

"The Eagle" soars through the air at the Olympics.

Makes Sense!

Eddie the Eagle was so popular that he received many endorsement deals. One was with Eagle Airlines.

Swim like an Eel

Eric "the Eel" Moussambani (moo-sahm-bah-NEE) followed in Edwards's footsteps. Moussambani represented Equatorial Guinea. He entered the 2000 Summer Olympics through a wildcard program for athletes from poor countries.

Moussambani trained early in the morning in a tiny hotel pool. He also trained in lakes and rivers. He did not have a coach. Fishermen gave him swimming tips. The Olympian had never even seen a full-size pool before the Games.

He swam only one meet at the Olympics, against two other swimmers. They were both disqualified after a false start. That meant Moussambani swam by himself. His single lap in the pool was televised around the world.

The cheers of the crowd and his huge smile after the event were lasting reminders of what makes the Olympics so special.

From Athlete to Coach

Moussambani was 22 when he swam in the Olympics. He went on to become an IT engineer. In 2012, he was named the coach of Equatorial Guinea's national swim team.

Moussambani competes in the 100m Freestyle.

THINK LINK

The wildcard program Moussambani used to enter the Olympics is controversial. Some people think only the very best athletes should be at the Olympics. What is your opinion?

> What might be a better way to spread the Olympic spirit to countries that don't have strong programs in a particular sport?

> Should wealthy countries such as the United States be required to help athletes from countries like Equatorial Guinea? Why or why not?

Torch Relay

The torch relay is a dramatic part of every Olympics. The torch begins its journey in Olympia, Greece, and takes a winding path to the Olympic **venue**. The torch broadens the Olympic community by bringing the spirit of the Games wherever it goes.

At the opening ceremony, the torch is used to light a **cauldron** that burns throughout the Olympics.

The torch is lit with special mirrors that focus the sun. This is the same way the ceremonial torch was lit during the ancient Olympic Games. This map shows the torch relay from the 1996 Atlanta, Georgia, Olympics.

April 27:

The first torchbearer in the United States was Rafer Johnson. He lit the cauldron at the 1984 Olympics in Los Angeles. This made him the last torchbearer of the 1984 Olympics and the first U.S. torchbearer for the 1996 Olympics.

May 14–15:

More than 300 riders carried the flame on horseback between Colorado and Missouri. They re-created part of the historic Pony Express.

May 17:

American Indians paddled the flame on the Arkansas River in Wichita, Kansas.

May 28–30:

The torch traveled up the Mississippi River from St. Louis to Hannibal, Missouri, on a steamboat.

July 14:

Boxer Muhammad Ali was the last torchbearer at the 1996 Games, touching the torch to the cauldron at the climax of the opening ceremony.

July 4:

A **seaplane** carried the torch from Sarasota to Miami, Florida. The flame was kept safe in a special lantern.

Spreading the Olympic Spirit

The Paralympics and the Special Olympics both create community through competition. Athletes with disabilities compete in the Paralympics. It started in 1948 with a small archery competition. The athletes were veterans in wheelchairs. Since then, it has grown into a huge sporting event. Today, the Paralympics take place right after the Olympics, in the same city. Athletes use the same venues.

At the Summer Paralympics, athletes swim, ride bikes, and run. In some events, blind athletes are paired with seeing partners. Basketball and tennis are played in wheelchairs. Some sports are unique to the Paralympics. Goalball is one example. It's like soccer but modified for people who are blind. During the Winter Paralympics, athletes ski and skate. There is also wheelchair curling. This sport is only open to those who must use a wheelchair in their everyday lives.

A Young Champion

Eleanor Simmonds is a British swimmer who was born with dwarfism. She is the youngest Paralympian champion for her country. She was just 13 when she won two golds at the 2008 Paralympics.

A skier from Germany competes in one of the downhill events.

Parallel Games

The term *Paralympics* comes from the Greek word *para*. It means next to. The Paralympics are next to, or parallel to, the Olympics.

Chantal Petitclerc (peh-tee-CLAHR) is a famous Paralympian. She lost the use of her legs when she was 13. Four years later, she discovered wheelchair racing.

Petitclerc competed in five Paralympics. During her career, she won 14 gold medals. In 2008, she was named the Canadian female athlete of the year. She was the first Paralympian to win the award since its start in 1933. In 2016, she received another great honor. She was named to the Canadian Senate.

"These things are not just about elevators and ramps, but about opening the mind," she said. "It sends a message to people...you can do whatever you want."

The Greatest

American swimmer Trischa Zorn was born blind. During her long Paralympic career, she earned 55 medals, including 41 golds. She won gold medals in all four swimming strokes.

Always a Rider

Lis Hartel lost the use of her legs in 1944. But she could still ride and control a horse. In 1952 and 1956, she won silver medals at the Olympics in dressage, a riding event.

In 2008, Petitclerc wins the 400m race.

The Special Olympics are for people with intellectual disabilities. Events occur around the world and throughout the year. Kids as young as eight can compete. Sports include swimming, cycling, and soccer. Bowling is popular. So is **bocce**, which is on the rise.

In 2015, almost five million athletes participated in the Special Olympics. The games also had more than one million volunteers and coaches who helped with events around the world.

The motto of the Special Olympics is, "Let me win. But if I cannot win, let me be brave in the attempt." These words have special meaning for disabled people, but they can apply to any athlete!

One of a Kind

The Olympic Committee bars the use of the word *Olympic* by other groups or businesses. The Special Olympics is the only other organization in the world that is allowed to use the term.

Presidential Seal

Eunice Shriver started the Special Olympics. She was one of President John F. Kennedy's sisters. The games grew out of a summer camp she held in her backyard. The Kennedy family is still involved in the organization.

A competitor lifts during the 2011 Special Olympics.

The Rarest Medal

Since 1964, a total of 18 de Coubertin medals have been given. Most of these medals have gone to athletes. By comparison, at each Olympics, hundreds of gold medals are awarded!

Vanderlei de Lima

Celebrating the Olympic Spirit

Can sports make the world a better place? The Olympics do just that, creating bonds between athletes, fans, and even nations—and proving that de Coubertin was right. One way that the Olympics continue to honor de Coubertin's vision is by awarding the Pierre de Coubertin medal to people who **embody** the values of the Games.

Brazilian Vanderlei de Lima received the medal in 2004. He was leading the Olympic marathon that year when a **deranged** bystander attacked him. De Lima lost precious seconds. He lost his lead and finished in third place. De Lima did not complain. He did not blame the race's organizers. Instead, as he crossed the finish line, he blew kisses to the crowd.

In 2016, he was chosen to light the cauldron at the Rio Olympics. It was a great moment in Olympic history. It would have made de Coubertin proud!

Glossary

apartheid—a policy of racial segregation practiced in South Africa between 1948 and 1991

attentively—with great focus

bocce—a horseshoes-like sport that involves throwing and rolling balls toward a target

boycotted—refused to buy a product or attend an event as a way of showing disapproval or to force change

capsize—to turn a boat over

cauldron—at the Olympics, the place where the Olympic flame burns during the competition

compass—a tool used to find direction

decathletes—athletes in track and field whose contest has 10 events, including running, jumping, and throwing events

deranged—mentally unstable

dinghy—a very small, open boat usually without a motor

diversity—variety, especially in terms of people with different religious or ethnic backgrounds

embody—to be an example of something in visible form

forge—to create something strong and lasting

fortitude—courage or determination in the face of pain and misfortune

grueling—extremely difficult and tiring

gunpowder—an explosive substance used in guns and also to create fireworks

heat—in the Olympics, an early round of a competition to determine who continues in the event

pentathlon—a track and field contest with five events

philosophers—people who study big, important issues and sometimes creates ideas for how to live

seaplane—a special plane that can land and take off from water

sponsored—supported someone else, usually financially

unified—a complete, united whole

venue—a place where an event is held

Index

45

Check It Out!

Books

Carter, Caela. 2016. *Tumbling*. New York: Viking Books for Young Readers.

Douglas, Gabrielle. 2013. *Grace, Gold, and Glory: My Leap of Faith*. Grand Rapids, Michigan: Zondervan.

Feinstein, John. 2012. *Rush for the Gold: Mystery at the Olympics* (The Sports Beat, 6). New York: Alfred A. Knopf Books for Young Readers.

Johnson, Rafer. 1998. *The Best That I Can Be*. New York: Doubleday.

Videos

Barber, Steven C. dir. 2009. *Unbeaten*. Polaris Global Media.

Fletcher, Dexter, dir. 2016. *Eddie the Eagle*. 20th Century Fox.

Hudson, Hugh, dir. 1981. *Chariots of Fire*. Warner Bros.

O'Connor, Gavin, dir. 2004. *Miracle*. Walt Disney.

Websites

International Paralympic Committee. www.paralympic.org.

Olympians, The. www.theolympians.co.

Olympics. www.olympic.org.

Special Olympics. www.specialolympics.org.

Try It!

In the spirit of the Olympics, plan an athletic competition for your friends, class, neighborhood, or school. Come up with at least five original events for your competition.

- Choose a location for the competition. Make sure it's a large enough space for all of the events.

- Make a diagram showing where each event will take place.

- Create a schedule of events so that people can participate in more than one event.

- Design a flyer advertising your competition with the place, date, and time.

- If you have the opportunity, put on your competition with friends or family. Have an awards ceremony, and post results. Most importantly, make sure that your competition creates community instead of conflict.

About the Author

Ben Nussbaum lives in Arlington, Virginia, with his wife, two children, a red fish, and a white cat. He's worked with Disney and the Smithsonian Institution, among other organizations, and he was the founding editor of *USA Today's* newsstand magazine group. He is currently a freelance writer and editor.

His favorite Olympic events are the track and field relay races. He hopes that tug-of-war, an Olympic sport between 1904 and 1920, will be reinstated as an official event.